A PARENT WHO PRAYS

A Journal to Guide You in Praying For Your Children

Katie Warner

If the lungs of prayer and of the Word of God do not nourish the breath of spiritual life, we risk suffocating in the midst of a thousand daily cares. Prayer is the breath of the soul and of life.

-Pope Benedict XVI-

Dear fellow parents,

Perhaps there is no greater gift we can give our children than the gift of our prayers. As parents we, almost without thinking, nourish their bodies and their minds throughout our daily activities with them, but it is in praying fervently for our children that we can help the life of grace flourish within their souls, aiding God in transforming them into the children He desires them to be.

Prayer is powerful. We marvel at how the prayers of Saint Monica, mother of her wayward son, Augustine, worked in conjunction with the Holy Spirit to bring him back to the ways of the Lord and put him on the road to sainthood. We treasure the witness of Saints Louis and Zelie Martin, parents of Saint Therese of Lisieux, who lived their lives as a prayer to God and passionately prayed for their daughters, who all entered the religious life and lived extraordinarily faithful lives.

Sometimes life happens, and we aren't as intentional about praying for our children as we would like to be. Allow this simple prayer guide and journal to give you the motivation and tools you need to make praying for your children a priority this year—and always.

May Jesus remain ever close to our children's hearts, may our Blessed Mother always keep them under Her mantle, may St. Joseph be their heavenly guardian, and may their guardian angels always protect them.

Katie Warner
CatholicKatie.com

How to Use **A Parent Who Prays**

1. Once a week (put it on your schedule!), sit down with this journal and put yourself in God's presence. **Sit in silence** for a few minutes, allowing your other daily duties to take a back seat to the beautiful work of praying for your children for this relatively brief moment in time.
2. **Read the special intention for the week**, with accompanying Scripture, quote, or reflection, and pray for that special virtue or intention listed to grow, with God's grace, in your child(ren).
3. Write down and pray about any additional, **specific intentions** that are on the forefront of your mind related to your child(ren). (Examples: a problem they are having at school, a big decision they need to make, an emotional struggle they are going through, a health issue, a challenging relationship in their life, etc.)
4. **Continue to pray** for the week's special and specific intentions each day that week. Refer to your journal/guide as needed. When praying the prayer provided on the page, substitute your child's or children's name(s) to make the prayers more personal.
5. At the end of the week, **offer a spiritual bouquet** for your child(ren) by writing down any gifts of prayer you offered that week for their specific intentions and the special intention provided. (Consider planning ahead by writing these down and then checking off as completed.) Some examples of gifts of prayer include:
    *   Masses
    *   Rosaries, Chaplets, and Novenas
    *   Individual prayers: Our Father, Hail Mary, Glory Be, the Memorare, Angelus, or the Prayer to the Holy Family (on next page)
    *   Daily sufferings and frustrations
    *   Daily successes and joys
    *   Fasting

This prayer guide can certainly remain a private journal. However, if you choose to gift this to your child at any point in time, the collection of these weekly bouquets will no doubt be an amazing offering of love to them, allowing them to see how your unceasing prayers for them are one of the most important ways you care for them as a mother or father.

Pope Francis wrote in his apostolic exhortation *Amoris Laetitia* (On Love in the Family), "All of us are called to keep striving towards something greater than ourselves and our families, and every family must feel this constant impulse. Let us make this journey as families, let us keep walking together. What we have been promised is greater than we can imagine. May we never lose heart because of our limitations, or ever stop seeking that fullness of love and communion which God holds out before us."

Prayer to the Holy Family

Jesus, Mary and Joseph,
in you we contemplate
the splendor of true love; to you we turn with trust.

Holy Family of Nazareth,
grant that our families too
may be places of communion and prayer, authentic schools of the Gospel
and small domestic churches.

Holy Family of Nazareth,
may families never again experience violence, rejection and division;
may all who have been hurt or scandalized find ready comfort and healing.

Holy Family of Nazareth,
make us once more mindful
of the sacredness and inviolability of the family, and its beauty in God's plan.

Jesus, Mary and Joseph, Graciously hear our prayer. Amen.

(Amoris Laetitia, 325)

PURITY

Blessed are the pure in heart, for they shall see God.
–Matthew 5:8

We must be pure. I do not speak merely of the purity of the senses. We must observe great purity in our will, in our intentions, in all our actions. - Saint Peter Julian Eymard

This week's **specific intentions** for my child(ren):

Lord, I ask you to hear these special intentions, together with my petition for my children's ongoing growth in purity, and I humbly offer you the spiritual bouquet below. Please bind these prayers together with your grace, and allow my children to become holy models of purity—purity of heart, of mind, and of body—in their families and in our world, which is so in need of sons and daughters of God who are filled with purity.

My **spiritual bouquet** for this week:

FAITH

For truly, I say to you, if you have faith as a grain of mustard seed, you will say to this mountain, `Move from here to there,' and it will move; and nothing will be impossible to you. -Matthew 17:20

Faith is to believe what you do not see; the reward of this faith is to see what you believe. - Saint Augustine

This week's **specific intentions** for my child(ren):

Lord, I ask you to hear these special intentions, together with my petition for my children's ongoing growth in faith, and I humbly offer you the spiritual bouquet below. Please bind these prayers together with your grace, and allow my children to have a faith that stands strong amidst our culture's attempts to weaken it. Help them love to learn about their faith, so that through constantly expanding their knowledge of you, they can grow in love of you, too.

My **spiritual bouquet** for this week:

PEACE

And the peace of God, which passes all understanding, will keep your hearts and your minds in Christ Jesus.
–Philippians 4:7

Never be in a hurry; do everything quietly and in a calm spirit. Do not lose your inner peace for anything whatsoever, even if your whole world seems upset. - Saint Francis de Sales

This week's **specific intentions** for my child(ren):

Lord, I pray for these special intentions and for my children to grow in peace, and I humbly offer you the spiritual bouquet below. With the help of your grace, allow my children to live lives characterized by peace and not anxiety, handing over their worries to you. Help me to teach them how to see areas in their life where their peace of heart is being threatened, and then have the courage to make changes to restore your life-sustaining peace.

My **spiritual bouquet** for this week:

HUMILITY

Do nothing from selfishness or conceit, but in humility count others better than yourselves. –Philippians 2:3

Someone once asked St. Bernard of Clairvaux what the three most important virtues are. He famously replied, "Humility, humility and humility."

This week's **specific intentions** for my child(ren):

Lord, I pray for these special intentions and for my children to grow in humility, and I offer you the spiritual bouquet below. With the help of your grace, allow my children to become truly humble individuals, who do not seek acclaim or earthly glory, but faithfulness to you. Help them encourage others, rather than foster a spirit of pride or competitiveness. Give them the humility to recognize their weaknesses, and the grace to improve upon them.

My **spiritual bouquet** for this week:

GRATITUDE

Give thanks in all circumstances; for this is the will of God in
Christ Jesus for you. −1 Thessalonians 5:18

No duty is more urgent than that of returning thanks.
- St. Ambrose

This week's **specific intentions** for my child(ren):

Lord, I pray for these special intentions and for my children to
become more grateful, and I offer you the spiritual bouquet
below. With the help of your grace, help them grow ever
more appreciative of the blessings and gifts you have given
them. Help me teach them how to always offer prayers and
words of thanksgiving to you, and to express gratitude to
others frequently. I pray that they count their blessings more
than their complaints.

My **spiritual bouquet** for this week:

PATIENCE

Be still before the LORD, and wait patiently for him.
–Psalm 37:7

Patience attains all that it strives for. He who has God finds
he lacks nothing: God alone suffices. - St. Teresa of Avila

This week's **specific intentions** for my child(ren):

Lord, I pray for these special intentions and for my children to
grow in patience, and I offer you the spiritual bouquet
below. With the help of your grace, help them become
patient in waiting for both small things (like a snack or a
vacation) and big things (like their future vocation). Help
them learn how to extend greater patience to others and
learn how to be patient with themselves and with their faults.
Give them the patience that turns sinners into saints.

My **spiritual bouquet** for this week:

HOPE

For I know the plans I have for you, says the LORD, plans for welfare and not for evil, to give you a future and a hope.
–Jeremiah 29:11

Consult not your fears but your hopes and your dreams. Think not about your frustrations, but about your unfulfilled potential. Concern yourself not with what you tried and failed in, but with what it is still possible for you to do.
–Pope John XXIII

This week's **specific intentions** for my child(ren):

Lord, I pray for these special intentions and for my children to always have hope, and I offer you this spiritual bouquet. With the help of your grace, allow them to hold onto the hope that gives meaning to life and strength to push forward in adversity. Help them always embrace hope, which directs them to their *heavenly* destination and answers the burning desire of their hearts for happiness.

My **spiritual bouquet** for this week:

PRUDENCE

"I, wisdom, dwell in prudence." –Proverbs 8:12

Blessed the one...who is not anxious to speak, but who reflects prudently on what he is to say and the manner in which he is to reply. –St. Francis of Assisi

This week's **specific intentions** for my child(ren):

Lord, I pray for these special intentions and for my children to become more prudent, and I offer you the spiritual bouquet below. With the help of your grace, I pray that my children learn to apply reason and practical wisdom to their everyday decisions and actions—big or small—seeking counsel as needed, using good judgment, and being decisive when they know the right direction in which to move.

My **spiritual bouquet** for this week:

JUSTICE

When justice is done, it is a joy to the righteous, but dismay to evildoers. –Proverbs 21:15

The source of justice is not vengeance but charity.
-Saint Bridget of Sweden

This week's **specific intentions** for my child(ren):

Lord, I pray for these special intentions and for my children to become more just, and I offer you the spiritual bouquet below. With the help of your grace, please allow my children to always work to maintain and restore justice in the world around them—both in and outside the home. Strengthen their will to remain firm in giving what is owed to God (like worship) and to others (like the right to life).

My **spiritual bouquet** for this week:

TEMPERANCE

Do not follow your base desires, but restrain your appetites. – Sirach 18:30

Also, temper all your works with moderation, that is to say, all your abstinence, your fasting, your vigils, and your prayers, for temperance sustains your body and soul with the proper measure, lest they fail. –Saint Hildegard

This week's **specific intentions** for my child(ren):

Lord, I pray for these special intentions and for my children to practice temperance, and I offer you the spiritual bouquet below. With the help of your grace, I pray my children will learn to moderate their attraction to worldly pleasure, using material things in a way that is healthy and leads to not fleeting, but lasting happiness. Help them combat the culture's attempts to allure them toward instant gratification and excess.

My **spiritual bouquet** for this week:

FORTITUDE

The Lord is my strength and my song. –Psalm 118:14

The person with fortitude is one who perseveres in doing what his conscience tells him he ought to do...The strong man will at times suffer, but he stands firm; he may be driven to tears, but he will brush them aside. When difficulties come thick and fast, he does not bend before them. –Saint Josemaria Escrivá

This week's **specific intentions** for my child(ren):

Lord, I pray for these special intentions and for my children to posses the heroic virtue of fortitude, and I offer you the spiritual bouquet below. With the help of your grace, I pray that they will always stand firm amidst difficulties and never stray in their effort to pursue the good. When their lives get difficult, let them run toward you, and not away from you. Help them resist temptations and strive to live moral lives.

My **spiritual bouquet** for this week:

VOCATION

I therefore, a prisoner for the Lord, beg you to lead a life worthy of the calling to which you have been called.
–Ephesians 4:1

If you are what you should be, then you will set the world on fire. –Saint Catherine of Siena

This week's **specific intentions** for my child(ren):

Lord, I pray for these special intentions and for my children's vocations, and I offer you the spiritual bouquet below. You know their futures, and you hold them in the palm of your hand. May they be open to the plan that you have for them, which will no doubt put their gifts to best use, glorify you, and bring them the most fulfillment. Above all, help them to fulfill their ultimate vocation to *love*, whether that be in family life or religious life, and let them do their vocational work well.

My **spiritual bouquet** for this week:

GENEROSITY

In all things I have shown you that by so toiling one must help the weak, remembering the words of the Lord Jesus, how he said, "It is more blessed to give than to receive."
–Acts 20:35

Teach us to give and not to count the cost.
–St. Ignatius of Loyola

This week's **specific intentions** for my child(ren):

Lord, I pray for these special intentions and for my children to grow in generosity, and I offer you the spiritual bouquet below. Help them learn to be generous with their time, talent, and treasure. With your grace, help them see opportunities to be generous at home (for example, by helping siblings with projects or chores or by sharing toys) and outside the home (like by volunteering and contributing to charities).

My **spiritual bouquet** for this week:

PRAYER

And this is the confidence which we have in him, that if we ask anything according to his will he hears us. –1 John 5:14

Prayer is the place of refuge for every worry, a foundation for cheerfulness, a source of constant happiness, a protection against sadness.
-St. John Chrysostom

This week's **specific intentions** for my child(ren):

Lord, I pray for these special intentions and for my children to have an ever-deepening prayer life. By your grace, I pray that they may come to thirst for more time with you in prayer, always seeking a more intimate relationship and conversation with you, and prioritizing time to grow with you in silence, by prayer with Scripture, and by coming to treasure the great and many prayers of the Church.

My **spiritual bouquet** for this week:

CONFIDENCE

I can do all things in him who strengthens me.
–Philippians 4:13

Jesus, source of my life, sanctify me. Oh my strength, fortify me. My commander, fight for me. –Saint Faustina

This week's **specific intentions** for my child(ren):

Lord, I pray for these special intentions and for my children to grow in confidence as they grow in age, and I present you this spiritual bouquet below. Though there are many threats that try to steal their confidence in themselves and in you, Lord, help them turn to you for strength. Allow them to exhibit confidence in the abilities and gifts you've given them, in a spirit of humility rather than pride. Allow that confidence to create in them a healthy independence from us as parents, but still a firm dependence on you.

My **spiritual bouquet** for this week:

CHASTITY

For this is the will of God, your sanctification: that you abstain from unchastity. –1 Thessalonians 4:3

"Chastity is a difficult, long term matter; one must wait patiently for it to bear fruit, for the happiness of loving kindness which it must bring. But at the same time, chastity is the sure way to happiness." –Pope Saint John Paul II

This week's **specific intentions** for my child(ren):

Lord, I pray for these special intentions and for my children to be chaste, leading up to and throughout their lifelong vocations. My God, you know that this virtue is attacked ferociously in our culture today. Give my children the resolve to exhibit chastity in dress, in the media they consume, and in their relationships. Help them achieve the "successful integration of [their] sexuality" which will lead them to unity of body and spirit (CCC 2337).

My **spiritual bouquet** for this week:

EDUCATION

Keep hold of instruction, do not let go; guard her, for she is your life. –Proverbs 4:13

True education enables us to love life and opens us to the fullness of life. –Pope Francis

This week's **specific intentions** for my child(ren):

Lord, I pray for these special intentions and for my children's ongoing education. By your grace, instill in them a love for learning, regardless of their age. Help them desire to become life-long students, always increasing their knowledge and understanding of the world around them and of your truth, goodness, and beauty. Give me the wisdom to teach them the most important truths while they are in my care, and instill in them a desire to direct all of their educational pursuits to your greater glory.

My **spiritual bouquet** for this week:

FRIENDSHIP WITH MARY

[F]or he has regarded the low estate of his handmaiden. For behold, henceforth all generations will call me blessed. – Luke 1:48

The greatest saints, those richest in grace and virtue will be the most assiduous in praying to the most Blessed Virgin, looking up to her as the perfect model to imitate and as a powerful helper to assist them."
-Saint Louis de Montfort

This week's **specific intentions** for my child(ren):

Lord, I pray for these special intentions and for my children's relationship with our Blessed Mother. I know that Scripture and the saints demonstrate how having a close relationship with Mary will lead us closer to you. Help my children call upon her maternal intercession and allow them to see Our Lady as their special heavenly Mother, who is there to protect them, comfort them, and light the way toward you.

My **spiritual bouquet** for this week:

HONORING THE LORD'S DAY

Remember the sabbath day, to keep it holy. Six days you shall labor, and do all your work; but the seventh day is a sabbath to the LORD your God;...for in six days the LORD made heaven and earth... and rested the seventh day; therefore the LORD blessed the sabbath day and hallowed it. –Exodus 20:8-11

Repose, leisure, peace, belong among the elements of happiness. If we have not escaped from harried rush, from mad pursuit, from unrest, from the necessity of care, we are not happy. –Josef Pieper

This week's **specific intentions** for my child(ren):

Lord, I pray for these intentions and for my children to always honor the Lord's Day throughout their lives. By your grace and the observation of the example I set for them, help them to keep Sunday a day of rest, worship, play, relaxation, and leisure with those they love most. Our culture tempts us to work on Sundays; let them instead protect their Sundays with determination.

My **spiritual bouquet** for this week:

SACRAMENTAL LIFE

Do this in remembrance of me. –Luke 22:19

Holy communion is the shortest and safest way to Heaven. – Saint Pius X

So many people see the confessional as a place of defeat, but confession is a place of victory every single time. –Fr. Mike Schmitz

This week's **specific intentions** for my child(ren):

Lord, I pray for these special intentions, and for my children to have a deep devotion to the sacraments, and I humbly offer you this spiritual bouquet. Infuse my children with your sacramental grace, and help them develop a habit of receiving the Holy Eucharist and Reconciliation, so they can commune with you, be strengthened by you, and come to you for healing. Let your sacraments transform them into the people you are calling them to be.

My **spiritual bouquet** for this week:

ZEAL

Never flag in zeal, be aglow with the Spirit, serve the Lord.
–Romans 12:11

Zeal reveals to us all the difference between a world grown merely secular and old, and the youthfulness of Christian love. –Anthony Esolen

This week's **specific intentions** for my child(ren):

Lord, I pray for these special intentions, and for my children never to lack in zeal, and I offer you this spiritual bouquet. Give them a strong, action-oriented desire to advance in their spiritual lives and move in the direction of righteousness. By your grace, give them the diligence to put love into action and to strengthen their resolution to progress in virtue and sanctity, making their spiritual life a priority, even when other things threaten to monopolize their time or attention.

My **spiritual bouquet** for this week:

FAMILY FRIENDSHIPS

Train up a child in the way he should go, and when he is old he will not depart from it. —Proverbs 22:6

Living together is an art, a patient, beautiful, fascinating journey. It does not end once you have won each other's love... Rather, it is precisely there where it begins! —Pope Francis

This week's **specific intentions** for my child(ren):

Lord, I pray for these special intentions, and for my children's relationships within our family, and I offer you this spiritual bouquet. Please allow our family ties to be strong, and for peace and harmony to be present among siblings and between parents and children in our home. I pray that we can work to build a foundation of love and enjoyment of one another that lasts into our children's adulthoods.

My **spiritual bouquet** for this week:

OBEDIENCE

You shall therefore love the LORD your God, and keep his charge, his statutes, his ordinances, and his commandments always. –Deuteronomy 11:1

God is more pleased to behold the lowest degree of obedience, for His sake, than all other good works which you can possibly offer to Him. -Saint John of the Cross

This week's **specific intentions** for my child(ren):

Lord, I pray for these special intentions, and for my children to practice obedience, and I offer you this spiritual bouquet. Through your grace, allow them to see obedience as a beautiful virtue, even when our culture tries to make obedience seem unnecessary or burdensome. Help cultivate in them a desire to be obedient to God and His will and laws, obedient to His Church, and obedient to us as parents, as well as to authority figures who are deserving of their obedience.

My **spiritual bouquet** for this week:

TRUST

Trust in the LORD with all your heart...-Proverbs 3:5

If your trust is great, then My generosity will be without limit. – Jesus to Saint Faustina

This week's **specific intentions** for my child(ren):

Lord, I pray for these special intentions, and for my children to always have a deep trust in the Lord, and I offer you this spiritual bouquet. Whatever life throws at them, allow them to trust in your plan for them and in your ability to care for them. By your grace, allow them to learn how to abandon themselves more fully to your will and not fear for their future. I pray that my children may also trust in me as a parent, to counsel them, encourage them, and be a model of firm trust and faith in God myself.

My **spiritual bouquet** for this week:

CHARITY

So faith, hope, love abide, these three; but the greatest of these is love. –1 Corinthians 13:13

Charity is the form, mover, mother and root of all the virtues. - Saint Thomas Aquinas

This week's **specific intentions** for my child(ren):

Lord, I pray for these special intentions, and for my children to become models of the virtue of charity. May they look to Your example, as well as the Blessed Mother and so many great saints, who changed the world with their deep love. Allow love to radiate from them in a beautifully active way by their own free choices, bringing about powerful and transformative effects in their lives and others. Help them always remember that their hearts long for—and were made for—love: to love and to be loved, and that they can find the Source of Love in You, God, their Creator.

My **spiritual bouquet** for this week:

MEEKNESS

Put on then, as God's chosen ones, holy and beloved, compassion, kindness, lowliness, meekness, and patience, forbearing one another and, if one has a complaint against another, forgiving each other; as the Lord has forgiven you, so you also must forgive. –Colossians 3:12-13

Nothing is more powerful than meekness. For as fire is extinguished by water, so a mind inflated by anger is subdued by meekness. –St. John Chrysostom

This week's **specific intentions** for my child(ren):

Lord, I pray for these special intentions, and for my children to grow in meekness. With your grace, allow my children to become very good at moderating their anger and controlling resentment toward others, finding strength through submission to God. I pray that in situations that provoke them to anger or un-forgiveness, they instead keep their sense of peace in adversity.

My **spiritual bouquet** for this week:

JOY

Clap your hands, all peoples! Shout to God with loud songs of joy! –Psalm 47: 1

Joy is a net of love by which we catch souls.- Saint Teresa of Calcutta

This week's **specific intentions** for my child(ren):

Lord, I pray for these special intentions, and for my children to exhibit and possess great joy, and I offer you this spiritual bouquet. By your grace, may they always look for authentic, fulfilling happiness through relationship with you, rather than through money, possessions, fame, or other fleeting and earthly things. Fill them with joy to share with others, so they can become lights for you in our often-dark world.

My **spiritual bouquet** for this week:

WISDOM

To get wisdom is better than gold... - Proverbs 16:16

Dost thou hold wisdom to be anything other than truth, wherein we behold and embrace the supreme good? –St. Augustine

This week's **specific intentions** for my child(ren):

Lord, I pray for these special intentions, and for my children to possess the gift of wisdom, and I offer you this spiritual bouquet. By your grace, allow them to grow in this highest gift of the Holy Spirit, by which they will come to value the things we believe by faith. Help them to have the wisdom to live a holy life and value created things because of you who created them. I pray they will share their wisdom with others, too, so those they meet may learn and come to love the truth of the Christian faith as well.

My **spiritual bouquet** for this week:

FRIENDSHIP WITH THE SAINTS

And when he had taken the scroll, the four living creatures and the twenty-four elders fell down before the Lamb, each holding a harp, and with golden bowls full of incense, which are the prayers of the saints. –Revelation 5:8

Sanctity is beautiful! It is a beautiful way! The saints give us a message. They tell us: be faithful to the Lord, because the Lord does not disappoint! –Pope Francis

This week's **specific intentions** for my child(ren):

Lord, I pray for these special intentions, and for my children to develop strong friendships with the saints. Give them a desire to learn more about the lives of the saints, to ask for their intercession, and to live in imitation of their holiness. May they acquire special patron saints along their Christian walk, who can inspire them to remain faithful to God and radically change the world around them with their love.

My **spiritual bouquet** for this week:

CLOSENESS WITH THE ANGELS

See that you do not despise one of these little ones; for I tell you that in heaven their angels always see the face of my Father who is in heaven. –Matthew 18:10

In this way is he [the true Christian] always pure for prayer. He also prays in the society of angels... he is never out of their holy keeping. –Clement of Alexandria

This week's **specific intentions** for my child(ren):

Lord, I pray for these special intentions, and for my children to develop a closeness with God's angels. I pray that, in appropriate time, they may be aware of the spiritual battle between good and evil going on in our world, and call on the angels to help them in spiritual combat. May they have a strong bond with their guardian angel in particular, who is tasked with guarding, protecting, ruling, and guiding them through this sometimes-messy life.

My **spiritual bouquet** for this week:

KNOWLEDGE

An intelligent mind acquires knowledge, and the ear of the wise seeks knowledge. - Proverbs 18:15

We can't have full knowledge all at once. We must start by believing; then afterwards we may be led on to master the evidence for ourselves. –Saint Thomas Aquinas

This week's **specific intentions** for my child(ren):

Lord, I pray for these special intentions, and for my children to possess the gift of knowledge, and I offer you this spiritual bouquet. By your grace, allow them to have the ability to judge things according to the truths of the Catholic faith, and see circumstances in their lives as you see them. With this knowledge, may they also recognize your purpose for their lives.

My **spiritual bouquet** for this week:

KINDNESS

[A]s servants of God we commend ourselves in every way:... by purity, knowledge, forbearance, kindness, the Holy Spirit, genuine love... –2 Corinthians 6:4,6

Be the living expression of God's kindness—kindness in your face, kindness in your eyes, kindness in your smile, kindness in your warm greeting. –Saint Teresa of Calcutta

This week's **specific intentions** for my child(ren):

Lord, I pray for these special intentions, and for my children to become vessels of kindness, and I offer you this spiritual bouquet. By your grace, allow them to treat others as they would want to be treated (or better!) and always look for opportunities to extend a warm, loving, merciful and *kind* hand to anyone in need. I pray that they will be motivated to intentionally spread kindness at home and elsewhere in some small way, every day.

My **spiritual bouquet** for this week:

EVANGELIZATION

For if I preach the gospel, that gives me no ground for boasting. For necessity is laid upon me. Woe to me if I do not preach the gospel! –1 Corinthians 9:16

Every Christian is challenged, here and now, to be actively engaged in evangelization; indeed, anyone who has truly experienced God's saving love does not need much time or lengthy training to go out and proclaim that love.
–Pope Francis

This week's **specific intentions** for my child(ren):

Lord, I pray for these special intentions, and for my children to be fervent in their mission of evangelization, in which we are all called to participate at baptism. May they be filled with the joy and love of Jesus and the Gospel, and then be fervent in sharing it with others. I pray that my children will always have the courage and passion to share the faith with others, even when it's difficult or unpopular to do so.

My **spiritual bouquet** for this week:

UNDERSTANDING

[W]e look not to the things that are seen but to the things that are unseen; for the things that are seen are transient, but the things that are unseen are eternal.
–2 Corinthians 4:18

Understanding is the reward of faith. Therefore, seek not to understand that you may believe, but believe that you may understand. –Saint Augustine

This week's **specific intentions** for my child(ren):

Lord, I pray for these special intentions, and for my children to grow in understanding, and I offer you this spiritual bouquet on their behalf. Allow them to grasp, in some incomplete but beautiful way, the essence of your truth and the truths of their Catholic faith, so they can possess an unwavering conviction about what they believe.

My **spiritual bouquet** for this week:

MODESTY

Do you not know that your body is a temple of the Holy Spirit within you, which you have from God? You are not your own; you were bought with a price. So glorify God in your body. –1 Corinthians 6:19-20

Let your modesty be a sufficient incitement, yea, an exhortation to everyone to be at peace on their merely looking at you. –Saint Ignatius of Loyola

This week's **specific intentions** for my child(ren):

Lord, I pray for these special intentions, and for my children to be modest in thought, word, and dress, and I present to you this spiritual bouquet. By your grace, allow them to see and embrace modesty as a practice that upholds their spiritual dignity as your sons or daughters. Help increase in them a deep respect for the human person, so modesty becomes a natural corollary of that respect.

My **spiritual bouquet** for this week:

EMPATHY

Rejoice with those who rejoice, weep with those who weep.
–Romans 12:15

There are two forms of intelligence. One is of the mind, the other of the heart. In the moral sphere there can be no doubt that the empathy of the heart is incomparably more important than the photography of the mind. Through the mind we can know and understand, but through the heart we can love, serve, and change the world.
–Dr. Donald DeMarco

This week's **specific intentions** for my child(ren):

Lord, I pray for these special intentions, and for my children to possess great empathy. By your grace, allow them to enter into other people's feelings, needs, and sufferings. Our world—and our home—is full of souls in need of empathy. Help my children fill that need.

My **spiritual bouquet** for this week:

SELF-CONTROL

He who keeps his mouth and his tongue keeps himself out of trouble. - Proverbs 21:23

Look toward Heaven, where Jesus Christ is waiting for you with His saints! Be faithful in his love, and fight courageously for your souls. –Saint Felicity

This week's **specific intentions** for my child(ren):

Lord, I pray for these special intentions, and for my children to grow in self-control. Help my children overcome temptation and deny themselves things that could draw them away from you. Allow them to guard their words, which are often used without discretion, and to monitor their thoughts and actions, which, when uncontrolled, could harm themselves or others.

My **spiritual bouquet** for this week:

WORK & LEISURE

Commit your work to the LORD, and your plans will be established. -Proverbs 16:3

Leisure is only possible when we are at one with ourselves. We tend to overwork as a means of self-escape, as a way of trying to justify our existence. —Josef Pieper

This week's **specific intentions** for my child(ren):

Lord, I pray for these special intentions, and for my children to have a healthy and fulfilling relationship with both work and leisure. Whether it be work at school, in the home, or in a professional environment, allow my children to offer their labor to you, Lord, seeing the good that comes from meaningful work. By your grace, also help them to be restful and embrace leisure, avoiding the "workaholism" prevalent in our day so as to maximize time spent with people they love, doing the things they love.

My **spiritual bouquet** for this week:

PIETY

Not every one who says to me, `Lord, Lord,' shall enter the kingdom of heaven, but he who does the will of my Father who is in heaven. –Matthew 7:21

[Piety] indicates our belonging to God, our deep bond with him, a relationship that gives meaning to our whole life and keeps us resolute, in communion with him, even during the most difficult and troubled moments. –Pope Francis

This week's **specific intentions** for my child(ren):

Lord, I pray for these special intentions, and for my children to grow in piety, and I offer you this spiritual bouquet. By your grace, instill in them a burning desire to worship you and to serve you with their whole selves and lives. I pray that this worship and service stem not from merely a sense of duty, but because of their immense love for you.

My **spiritual bouquet** for this week:

FORGIVENESS

Then Peter came up and said to him, "Lord, how often shall my brother sin against me, and I forgive him? As many as seven times?" Jesus said to him, "I do not say to you seven times, but seventy times seven." –Matthew 18:21-22

He who knows how to forgive prepares for himself many graces from God. As often as I look upon the cross, so often will I forgive with all my heart. -St. Faustina

This week's **specific intentions** for my child(ren):

Lord, I pray for these special intentions, and for my children to learn to forgive well and often, and I offer you this spiritual bouquet. By your grace, help them learn to extend forgiveness when it is uncomfortable or when it seems impossible, recognizing the ultimate example of forgiveness you have provided for us, when even on the cross you forgave your enemies who put you to death.

My **spiritual bouquet** for this week:

HEALTH & SAFETY

Beloved, I pray that all may go well with you and that you may be in health; I know that it is well with your soul.
–3 John 1:2

This week's **specific intentions** for my child(ren):

Lord, I pray for these special intentions, and for my children's health and safety. God, this world can be scary and cruel, and sometimes innocent young souls experience violence and pain that we can only pray they might never endure. I ask that, through your mercy, you protect them from serious illness and harm. Should they experience pain or be in a dangerous situation, send your host of angels to be with them, and give them the grace to endure anything they may battle. Finally, when I am tempted to be fearful or let my imagination run wild, whisper in my heart a reminder to trust in you, knowing you love my children even more.

My **spiritual bouquet** for this week:

Fear God, and keep his commandments; for this is the whole duty of man. –Ecclesiastes 12:13

For the absence of the fear of God is arrogance and pride. How dare sinners sashay up to God as a chum without first falling down in repentance and fear and calling on the Blood of Christ to save us? –Dr. Peter Kreeft

This week's **specific intentions** for my child(ren):

Lord, I pray for these special intentions, and for my children to grow in the Holy Spirit's gift of fear of the Lord, and I offer you this spiritual bouquet. By your grace, instill in them a desire never to offend you, either in word or deed, my God, and the confidence that you will give them the grace to make this possible. Fill them with awe and wonder of you, which allows them to respect you out of their deep love.

My **spiritual bouquet** for this week:

GENTLENESS

But the wisdom from above is first pure, then peaceable, gentle, open to reason, full of mercy and good fruits, without uncertainty or insincerity. –James 3:17

Nothing is so strong as gentleness, nothing so gentle as real strength. –Saint Francis de Sales

This week's **specific intentions** for my child(ren):

Lord, I pray for these special intentions, and for my children to grow in gentleness, and I offer you this spiritual bouquet. By your grace and through my teaching, allow my children to learn how to act calmly and politely toward others. I pray that others may characterize them by their humility and thankfulness toward you. I also ask, Lord, that you give them the strength to correct and accept corrections *gently,* humbly, and lovingly.

My **spiritual bouquet** for this week:

RELATIONSHIP WITH FRIENDS

There are friends who pretend to be friends, but there is a friend who sticks closer than a brother.
—Proverbs 18:24

There is nothing on this earth more to be prized than true friendship. —Saint Thomas Aquinas

This week's **specific intentions** for my child(ren):

Lord, I pray for these special intentions, and for my children to have strong, *good* friendships. I know the impact that friends can have on my children. A good friend can lead them toward a life of virtue, and a bad friend can lead them down paths of vice. By your grace, lead my children toward friends with good character, who encourage them to be more like the people you desire them to be. Also, I pray that my children always *be* good friends to others, so their friends may see in them a reflection of you.

My **spiritual bouquet** for this week:

COUNSEL

The wisdom of a prudent man is to discern his way, but the folly of fools is deceiving. –Proverbs 14:8

Nothing is so strong as gentleness, nothing so gentle as real strength. –Saint Francis de Sales

This week's **specific intentions** for my child(ren):

Lord, I pray for these special intentions, and for my children to possess the Holy Spirit's gift of counsel, and I offer you this spiritual bouquet. By your grace, help my children learn to judge how best to act in any situation, calling on the Holy Spirit's guidance. I pray they will defend the truths of the faith, always living according to them as a faithful disciple of yours. May their good counsel serve also as a witness to others, so they may inspire friends to also act prudently.

My **spiritual bouquet** for this week:

SOLICITUDE

Love one another with brotherly affection; outdo one another in showing honor. –Romans 12:10

What is the mark of love for your neighbor? Not to seek what is for your own benefit, but what is for the benefit of the one loved, both in body and in soul. –St. Basil

This week's **specific intentions** for my child(ren):

Lord, I pray for these special intentions, and for my children to grow in solicitude, and I offer you this spiritual bouquet. By your grace, help them exhibit great "brotherly love," by demonstrating care and concern for the wellbeing of those around them. Rather than being envious, I pray they will admire the skills and accomplishments of others, and excel at congratulating and encouraging the people you place in their path.

My **spiritual bouquet** for this week:

INDEPENDENCE

[A]nd I shall walk at liberty, for I have sought thy precepts.
–Psalm 119:45

Freedom consists not in doing what we like, but in having the right to do what we ought. –Pope Saint John Paul II

This week's **specific intentions** for my child(ren):

Lord, I pray for these special intentions, and for my children to become strong, independent adults. By your grace, allow my children to learn how to exercise their own freedom and independence from us as parents, at the appropriate time as they grow up, and then bestow them with the ability to make good decisions to care for themselves, exercising the freedom to choose what is right. I pray that they may always maintain a healthy relationship with us, compatible with their mature freedom.

My **spiritual bouquet** for this week:

GOODNESS

Surely goodness and mercy shall follow me all the days of my life; and I shall dwell in the house of the LORD forever.
–Psalm 23:6

A morally good act requires the goodness of its object, of its end, and of its circumstances together. –Catechism of the Catholic Church 1760

This week's **specific intentions** for my child(ren):

Lord, I pray for these special intentions, and for my children to possess the Holy Spirit's fruit of goodness, and I offer you this spiritual bouquet. By your grace, Lord, allow my children to honor you by doing what is right. Help them to avoid sin and make morally good choices, a demonstration of their love for you and a response of gratitude for *your* great goodness toward us.

My **spiritual bouquet** for this week:

SELF-AWARENESS

Examine yourselves, to see whether you are holding to your faith. Test yourselves. Do you not realize that Jesus Christ is in you? - unless indeed you fail to meet the test!
–2 Corinthians 13:5

Know thyself, and thy faults, and thus live." —St. Augustine

This week's **specific intentions** for my child(ren):

Lord, I pray for these special intentions, and for my children to exhibit great self-awareness. By your grace, Lord, I pray my children will always aspire to self-improvement, being aware of their faults and actively seeking to uproot them and grow in holiness. Enlighten them to recognize when they are far from you. Also, help them to be aware of their virtues and talents, rejoicing in them as gifts that come from you, and exercising them for your glory.

My **spiritual bouquet** for this week:

RESPECT FOR LIFE

You shall not kill. –Exodus 20:13

"Before I formed you in the womb I knew you, and before you were born I consecrated you... --Jeremiah 1:5

The fundamental human right, the presupposition of every other right, is the right to life itself...from the moment of conception until its natural end. –Pope Benedict XVI

This week's **specific intentions** for my child(ren):

Lord, I pray for these special intentions, and for my children to always have a deep respect for life. By their words and actions, Lord, help my children be passionately pro-life, believing in the sanctity of all human life from conception to natural death, and be open to life in their own future families. Inspire them to defend life issues at home and publically, even when it is unpopular to do so.

My **spiritual bouquet** for this week:

MEANINGFUL SUFFERING

I consider that the sufferings of this present time are not worth comparing with the glory that is to be revealed to us. – Romans 8:18

If God sends you many sufferings, it is a sign that He has great plans for you and certainly wants to make you a saint. -St. Ignatius Loyola

This week's **specific intentions** for my child(ren):

Lord, I pray for these special intentions, and for my children to suffer with dignity. Though it breaks a parent's heart to see a child suffer, I ask that when they do, you infuse them with grace in moments of suffering, allowing them to see the redemptive power in them. I pray that my children will offer up their pain and unite their sufferings with yours on the cross, never thinking their suffering is meaningless.

My **spiritual bouquet** for this week:

SANCTITY

You, therefore, must be perfect, as your heavenly Father is perfect. –Matthew 5:48

Life holds only one tragedy: not to have been a saint. –Léon Bloy

This week's **specific intentions** for my child(ren):

Lord, I pray for these special intentions, and for my children to be saints in heaven someday, and I offer you this spiritual bouquet. More than any other prayer intention, Lord, I implore you to mold my children into great saints. May they come to see that you are calling them to the heights of holiness, no matter what state or vocation in life they may find themselves in. Help them to see small ways to grow in sanctity every day and be fervent in taking those little steps to draw closer to you and become more like you, so they may spend eternity with you in the company of your saints.

My **spiritual bouquet** for this week:

In the family of prayer,
in strong moments and in difficult periods,
may we be entrusted to one another,
in order that every one of us in the family may be
protected by God's love.

-Pope Francis-

Thank you, fellow parents, for joining me on this special prayer journey for our children. May you always turn to prayer as the source of healing for your children's past, a wellspring of grace for their present, and a fountain of hope for their future.

Please recommend this prayer journal to others,
and share your feedback with me at

CatholicKatieOnline@gmail.com

You can also find me and other great resources to help your family live a more intentional and spiritual life at **CatholicKatie.com** and on Facebook at Facebook.com/ CatholicKatieOnline.

Made in the USA
Columbia, SC
28 December 2018